YOUR KNOWLEDGE HAS VALUE

AF141562

- We will publish your bachelor's and
  master's thesis, essays and papers

- Your own eBook and book -
  sold worldwide in all relevant shops

- Earn money with each sale

Upload your text at www.GRIN.com
and publish for free

Uqbah Iqbal

The History of the Look-To-Israel Idea in Malaysia (1957-2003)

GRIN Publishing

Bibliographic information published by the German National Library:

The German National Library lists this publication in the National Bibliography; detailed bibliographic data are available on the Internet at http://dnb.dnb.de .

Imprint:

Copyright © 2015 GRIN Verlag GmbH
Print and binding: Books on Demand GmbH, Norderstedt Germany
ISBN: 978-3-656-94270-2

This book at GRIN:

http://www.grin.com/en/e-book/296038/the-history-of-the-look-to-israel-idea-in-malaysia-1957-2003

GRIN - Your knowledge has value

Since its foundation in 1998, GRIN has specialized in publishing academic texts by students, college teachers and other academics as e-book and printed book. The website www.grin.com is an ideal platform for presenting term papers, final papers, scientific essays, dissertations and specialist books.

THE HISTORY OF THE LOOK-TO-ISRAEL IDEA IN MALAYSIA (1957-2003)

Introduction

When it's a matter of relations with Israel, the Malaysian government such as on the horns because any incident could impact the government's image in the eyes of the people. A brief review of Malaysia-Israel relations historiography reveals that while there is a large amount of literature on the negative aspects between the two countries, not much is written about the positive aspects of the past, bringing to the Look-To-Israel idea. This study will examine the extent of the Malaysian government's acceptance against Israeli involvement in this country, the sectors involved, contributing to the importance of this study because it identifies the scale and scope of the relationship between Israel and Malaysia despite the absence of diplomatic relations over the years. Answers to these questions will provide the basis for determining and understanding the level of relations between the Israeli government and the Malaysian government.

The method used in this study is based on the newspaper research methods in the National Library of Singapore and the National Archives of Malaysia that encourage the Look-To-Israel idea. 1957 was chosen as the starting year of the study because it is the period of Tunku Abdul Rahman's administration as the Malaysia's first Prime Minister, while 2003 was chosen as the closing year because it is the final year of the Malaysia's fourth Prime Minister administration, Tun Dr. Mahathir Mohamad. Through the reading of other studies, researcher found that there are only two previous studies that touched on the relationship between Malaysia and Israel in depth, namely Moshe Yegar[1] which touched on the Look-To-Israel idea in complete from the time of Tunku Abdul Rahman until the time of Tun Dr. Mahathir Mohamad's administration and Jacob Abadi.[2] This study will complement the two studies through the use of different primary sources. Researcher can use it as a background to the study.

The Look-To-Israel Idea

---

[1] Moshe Yegar, Malaysia: Anti-Semitism without Jews in *Jewish Political Studies Review* 18: 3-4, 2006.
[2] Jacob Abadi, *Israel's Quest for Recognition and Acceptance in Asia: Garrison State Diplomacy*, London, Frank Cass, 2003.

For starters, Israeli dealers feel optimistic after the establishment of Malaysia, the coming years will bring more trade opportunities to them in this country. Astraco Asia Trading Co. Ltd. manager, H. Lissauer said they felt with the formation of Malaysia, the region will enter a period of rapid development and prosperity. This company is the sole organization in Singapore to manage the affairs of the trade between 50 Israeli companies with the Federation of Malaya. The value of trade between Israel and the Federation of Malaya by 1962 is small. But it still increased from $ 1.7 million in 1960 to $3 million in 1961. The main import of Israel from the Federation of Malaya was rubber. Purchase price of these commodities has increased from $ 440,000 in 1960 to $ 700,000 in 1961. In addition to buying directly from the Federation of Malaya, Israel also buying more rubber from this country through the broker in London.[3] When Singapore formed Malaysia, its government establish close ties with Israel. On December 11, 1964, members of the opposition question the existence of a youth exchange program initiated by the government of Singapore and Israel in 1963. There were also Israeli representatives who were invited to come to the seminars in Malaysia by the United Nations.[4]

When he was the President of the Asian Football Confederation in 1958, Tunku Abdul Rahman associated closely with the Football Association of Israel, especially during the final round of the Asian Football Cup in Israel in 1964.[5] On 26 November 1964, Tunku Abdul

---

[3] Anonymous, Israel's Malaysia hopes. SHE SEES GOOD IMMEDIATE PROSPECTS FOR HER VARIOUS GARMENTS AND CANNED FOODSTUFFS in *The Straits Times*, 14 September 1962, p. 16.

[4] Our Parliamentary Reporters, Relations with Israel? Denial by Tengku and a word of caution... Opposition MPs warned of the risk of 'a lot of misunderstanding' with Arab countries in *The Straits Times*, 12 December 1964, p. 8.

[5] File of Jabatan Arkib Negara Malaysia, *Unforgettable Moments Recorded During- The Asian Football Cup Finals - 1964 Presented To Tunku Abdul Rahman Putra (President, A.F.C. by The Israel Football Association, Tel - Aviv, 3.6.1964.*, Para pengurus dan pemain-pemain yang mengambil bahagian selamat tiba di Tel -AAviv pada 3.6.1964.Bagi The Asian Football Cup Finals 1964, 3 June 1964. See also file of Jabatan Arkib Negara Malaysia, *Unforgettable Moments Recorded During- The Asian Football Cup Finals - 1964 Presented To Tunku Abdul Rahman Putra (President, A.F.C. by The Israel Football Association, Tel - Aviv, 3.6.1964.*, Para Pengurus dan pemain dari Korea yang mengambil bahagian Teh Asia Football Cup di Tel-Aviv pada 3.6.1964 selamat mendarat di negara itu dan disambut dengan jambangan bunga., 3 June 1964. See also file of Jabatan Arkib Negara Malaysia, *Unforgettable Moments Recorded During- The Asian Football Cup Finals - 1964 Presented To Tunku Abdul Rahman Putra (President, A.F.C. by The Israel Football Association, Tel - Aviv, 3.6.1964.*, Pasukan yang mengambil bahagian - The Asian Football Cup Finals bergambar ramai di Tel - Aviv, 3.5.1964., 3 May 1964. See also file of Jabatan Arkib Negara Malaysia, *Unforgettable Moments Recorded During- The Asian Football Cup Finals - 1964 Presented To Tunku Abdul Rahman Putra (President, A.F.C. by The Israel Football Association, Tel - Aviv, 3.6.1964.*, Tan Sri Hamzah Abu Samah bergambar dengan pengurus-pengurus pasukan yang mengambil bahagian - The Asian Football Cup Finals - Tel-Aviv pada 3.6.1964., 3 June 1964. See also file of Jabatan Arkib Negara Malaysia, *Unforgettable Moments Recorded*

2

Rahman stated that Malaysia's recognition of Israel only to the country and not on the government of Israel. The Malaysian government does not intend to recognize the state of

During- The Asian Football Cup Finals - 1964 Presented To Tunku Abdul Rahman Putra (President, A.F.C. by The Israel Football Association, Tel - Aviv, 3.6.1964., Wakil-wakil Pengurus bagi negara yang mengambil bahagian bergambar ramai di pejabat semasa The Asian Football Cup Finals, Tel-Aviv, 3.6.1964., 3 June 1964. See also file of Jabatan Arkib Negara Malaysia, *Unforgettable Moments Recorded During- The Asian Football Cup Finals - 1964 Presented To Tunku Abdul Rahman Putra (President, A.F.C. by The Israel Football Association, Tel - Aviv, 3.6.1964.*, Pengurus-pengurus bagi negara-negara yang mengambil bahagian bergambar ramai di Dewan ketika menghadiri The Asian Football Cup Finals 1964 di Tel -Aviv., no date. See also file of Jabatan Arkib Negara Malaysia, *Unforgettable Moments Recorded During- The Asian Football Cup Finals - 1964 Presented To Tunku Abdul Rahman Putra (President, A.F.C. by The Israel Football Association, Tel - Aviv, 3.6.1964.*, Pengurus dari Tel Aviv sedang bercakap semasa wakil-wakil negara hadir bagi The Asian Football Cup Final pada tahun 1964., no date. See also file of Jabatan Arkib Negara Malaysia, *Unforgettable Moments Recorded During- The Asian Football Cup Finals - 1964 Presented To Tunku Abdul Rahman Putra (President, A.F.C. by The Israel Football Association, Tel - Aviv, 3.6.1964.*, Pengurus-pengurus dari negara-negara yang mengambil bahagian bergambar ramai semasa berkumpul di Tel-Aviv pada 1964 bagi The Asian Football Cup Finals., no date. See also file of Jabatan Arkib Negara Malaysia, *Unforgettable Moments Recorded During- The Asian Football Cup Finals - 1964 Presented To Tunku Abdul Rahman Putra (President, A.F.C. by The Israel Football Association, Tel - Aviv, 3.6.1964.*, Pegawai-pegawai bagi negara-negara yang mengambil bahagian The Asian Football Cup Finals 1964 di Tel Aviv bergambar ramai sebagai kenang-kenangan., no date. See also file of Jabatan Arkib Negara Malaysia, *Unforgettable Moments Recorded During- The Asian Football Cup Finals - 1964 Presented To Tunku Abdul Rahman Putra (President, A.F.C. by The Israel Football Association, Tel - Aviv, 3.6.1964.*, Pengurus-pengurus yang mengambil bahagian The Asian Football Cup Finals 1964 sedang berbincang, no date. See also file of Jabatan Arkib Negara Malaysia, *Unforgettable Moments Recorded During- The Asian Football Cup Finals - 1964 Presented To Tunku Abdul Rahman Putra (President, A.F.C. by The Israel Football Association, Tel - Aviv, 3.6.1964.*, Tan Sri Hamzah Abu Samah sedang bersantai bersama-sama dengan rakan-rakan di Tel-Aviv pada 1964, sempena The Asian Football Cup Finals., no date. See also file of Jabatan Arkib Negara Malaysia, *Unforgettable Moments Recorded During- The Asian Football Cup Finals - 1964 Presented To Tunku Abdul Rahman Putra (President, A.F.C. by The Israel Football Association, Tel - Aviv, 3.6.1964.*, Pasukan Korea dan lawannya sedang beraksi dipadang sempena The Asian Football Cup Finals di Tel Aviv pada 1964., no date. See also file of Jabatan Arkib Negara Malaysia, *Unforgettable Moments Recorded During- The Asian Football Cup Finals - 1964 Presented To Tunku Abdul Rahman Putra (President, A.F.C. by The Israel Football Association, Tel - Aviv, 3.6.1964.*, Pemain-pemain yang mengambil bahagian sedang beraksi di padang dalam perlawanan The Asian Football Cup Finals di Tel - Aviv 1964., no date. See also file of Jabatan Arkib Negara Malaysia, *Unforgettable Moments Recorded During- The Asian Football Cup Finals - 1964 Presented To Tunku Abdul Rahman Putra (President, A.F.C. by The Israel Football Association, Tel - Aviv, 3.6.1964.*, Bendera-bendera yang mengambil bahagian dalam The Asian Football Cup Finals - 1964 di Tel-Aviv sedang dijulang sempena perasmian., no date. See also file of Jabatan Arkib Negara Malaysia, *Unforgettable Moments Recorded During- The Asian Football Cup Finals - 1964 Presented To Tunku Abdul Rahman Putra (President, A.F.C. by The Israel Football Association, Tel - Aviv, 3.6.1964.*, Bendera-bendera negara yang mengambil bahagian diarak keliling padang sempena perasmian The Asian Football Cup Finals - 1964 di Tel - Aviv., no date. See also file of Jabatan Arkib Negara Malaysia, *Unforgettable Moments Recorded During- The Asian Football Cup Finals - 1964 Presented To Tunku Abdul Rahman Putra (President, A.F.C. by The Israel Football Association, Tel - Aviv, 3.6.1964.*, Bendera-bendera yang mengambil bahagian sedang berkibar di tengah padang sempena perasmian The Asian Football Cup Finals 1964 di Tel-Aviv., no date. See also file of Jabatan Arkib Negara Malaysia, *Unforgettable Moments Recorded During- The Asian Football Cup Finals - 1964 Presented To Tunku Abdul Rahman Putra (President, A.F.C. by The Israel Football Association, Tel - Aviv, 3.6.1964.*, Pasukan yang berjaya sedang menjulang piala dan mengibar bendera mengelilingi padang sempena The Asian Football Cup Finals - 1964., no date. See also file of Jabatan Arkib Negara Malaysia, *Unforgettable Moments Recorded During- The Asian Football Cup Finals - 1964 Presented To Tunku Abdul Rahman Putra (President, A.F.C. by The Israel Football Association, Tel - Aviv, 3.6.1964.*, Pemain No. 8 sedang menerima hadiah dalam perlawanan The Asian Football Cup Finals - 1964 di Tel - Aviv., no date. See also file of Jabatan Arkib Negara Malaysia, *Unforgettable Moments Recorded During- The Asian Football Cup Finals - 1964 Presented To Tunku Abdul Rahman Putra (President, A.F.C. by The Israel Football Association, Tel - Aviv, 3.6.1964.*, Pasukan dari India sedang menjulang piala kemenangan dan bergambar ramai sempena The Asian Football Cup Finals - 1964 di Tel- Aviv., no date.

Israel as a kingdom as long as the Alliance Government holds the power. The Malaysian government gave recognition to the state of Israel as it exists as an outcome decision from the United Nations. Due to the government's policy in supporting the United Nations and its Charter, then Malaysia give this recognition. According to international law, the recognition of a country cannot be withdrawn unless happen any events that brought the country no longer exist.[6] Israeli businessmen who come to Malaysia is allowed only for business purposes and not involved in political affairs.[7] On 26 November 1965, Tunku Abdul Rahman reminded the Pan-Malaysian Islamic Party members not to make allegations that are unfounded against the government regarding Israel so that no Arab countries severed ties with Malaysia.[8]

On May 14, 1966, the Chief Minister of Kelantan, Dato' Haji Mohamed Asri Haji Muda said he will meet the Acting Prime Minister, Tun Abdul Razak to submit proposals in improving the image of Malaysia among Afro-Asia countries. This is because he believes the image of Malaysia declined when the Malaysian government recognizes Israel.[9] Earlier this view also expressed by United Malays National Organisation (UMNO) Arau branch on March 13, 1965[10] to provide hope for Malaysia get a seat in the National Conference of Asia-Africa in June 1965.[11] On August 24, 1966, Tunku Abdul Rahman stated Malaysia recognizes the existence of the state of Israel because it becomes the United Nations member same like Malaysia's recognition to the Communist countries, although there are no diplomatic relations with them. The government does not need to recall the recognition of Israel as there is no reason to do so. This is because Malaysia has never recognized the Israeli

---

[6] Anonymous, 'KERAJAAN' ISRAEL BELUM DI-I'TIRAF in *Berita Harian*, 26 November 1964, p. 5. See also Firdaus Abdullah & Allas Ali, 'KITA ANTI-KEKERASAN'. Tengku menerangkan: Kita mengakui Israel tapi tidak ada perhubongan in *Berita Harian*, 4 December 1964, p. 5.
[7] Anonymous, MENGAPA SAUDAGAR ISRAEL DI-SUROH KELUAR in *Berita Harian*, 22 March 1966, p. 5. See also Anonymous, Israeli trader is expelled. He indulged in local politics, says Tengku in *The Straits Times*, 13 January 1966, p. 1. See also Abul Fazil, Allegations not true, says Israeli businessman in *The Straits Times*, 14 January 1966, p. 11.
[8] Mazlan Nordin, Tengku kecham pemimpin2 PAS di-Dewan Ra'ayat . Jangan membuat tudohan bukan2 atas dasar luar in *Berita Harian*, 26 November 1965, p. 5. See also Anonymous, Hubongan dgn Israel: Amaran kpd pembangkang. 'Tudohan2 liar boleh menimbulkan salah faham yg menyukarkan' in *Berita Harian*, 12 December 1964, p. 5. See also Our Parliamentary Reporters, Relations with Israel? Denial by Tengku and a word of caution... Opposition MPs warned of the risk of 'a lot of misunderstanding' with Arab countries in *The Straits Times*, 12 December 1964, p. 8.
[9] Anonymous, Imej Malaysia: Asri hendak berjumpa Tun in *Berita Harian*, 14 May 1966, p. 3. See also Anonymous, PAS na' minta tarek akuan kpd Israel in *Berita Harian*, 13 August 1964, p. 5.
[10] Anonymous, Seruan menarek balek pengakuan kapada Israel in *Berita Harian*, 14 March 1965, p. 10. See also Anonymous, 'Withdraw Israel recognition' in *The Straits Times*, 14 March 1965, p. 7.
[11] Anonymous, UMNO Arau seru pengakuan kepada Israel di-batalkan in *Berita Harian*, 26 March 1965, p. 8.

government although acknowledge the existence of the state of Israel. Malaysia has also no relations with Israel and did not intend to establish diplomatic relations among both countries. Tunku Abdul Rahman rejected the opposition's notion that Malaysia's attitude regarding Israel was not pleasant Arab countries.[12]

On June 11, 1967, Assistant Secretary of UMNO, Hassan bin Haji Mohamed urged UMNO members in Malaysia to learn from Israel's victory in the Middle East War. Although the number of their people is little but they can easily beat Arab countries because they are stronger unified. Arab parties also easy to break.[13] By the year 1974, Malaysia imported fertilizers and oranges from Israel and exporting rubber and tin into the country.[14] On March 28, 1979, the Malaysian government welcomed the peace treaty between Egypt and Israel as a first step towards a comprehensive solution to the problems of the Middle East.[15] On 18 April 1985, TV3, the only Malaysian commercial channels broadcast a film about the life of Israeli Prime Minister, Golda Meir.[16]

The Foreign Minister of Malaysia, Dato' Rais Yatim, explained on December 5, 1986 that the Malaysian government is against Zionism policy and not the existence of the Jewish people or Israel as a state, as assumed by some foreign countries. This is following the Malaysian government protests over the visit of President of Israel, Chaim Herzog to Singapore at the end of last month.[17] Previously on 8 November 1986, he stated that the Malaysian government will not be recalled its High Commissioner to Singapore during the visit of Chaim Herzog. Such action is not wise though Malaysians feel disappointed with the visit.[18] Prime Minister, Dato' Seri Dr. Mahathir Mohamad also said that the Malaysian

---

[12] Thalatha, Malaysia tidak pernah akui negara Israel in *Berita Harian*, 24 August 1966, p. 5. See also Anonymous, OUR TIES WITH ARAB NATIONS ALWAYS CORDIAL: TENGKU in *The Straits Times*, 24 August 1966, p. 5.

[13] Anonymous, BELAJAR-LAH DARI ISRAEL, KATA TOKOH UMNO in *Berita Harian*, 11 June 1967, p. 1.

[14] Anonymous, Imports from Israel almost at standstill in *The Straits Times*, 8 March 1974, p. 17.

[15] Anonymous, Malaysia hails pact in *The Straits Times*, 28 March 1979, p. 3.

[16] Anonymous, Sorry about that — TV3 in *The Straits Times*, 18 April 1985, p. 40.

[17] Anonymous, Malaysia hanya tentang Zionisme in *Berita Harian*, 6 December 1986, p. 1. See also Anonymous, Malaysia opposes Zionism, not Israel or Jewish people, says Rais Yatim in *The Business Times*, 6 December 1986, p. 12. See also Anonymous, Rais: Govt opposes Zionism, not Jews in *The Straits Times*, 6 December 1986, p. 13. See also Anonymous, Johor 'has no mandate to decide on ties review' in *The Straits Times*, 20 November 1986, p. 13.

[18] Anonymous, KL tak akan bertindak in *Berita Harian*, 9 November 1986, p. 2. See also Anonymous, 'KL won't recall envoy during Herzog visit' in *The Straits Times*, 8 November 1986, p. 30. See also Anonymous, KL-Singapore relations intact, assures Dr M in *The Business Times*, 17 November 1986, p. 1. See also Anonymous, Republic should heed Malaysians' views: Hussein in *The Straits Times*, 19 November 1986, p. 12.

government has no right to object Chiam Herzog visits to Singapore. This is because the matter involves the sovereignty of Singapore.[19] As an independent nation, Singapore is free to make their own decisions.[20] Chairman of the People's Action Committee (PAC), Dr. Usman Awang stated that the demonstrations in Malaysia for opposing Chaim Herzog visit to Singapore is aimed against Zionism and not against the Chinese in Singapore.[21]

The Malaysian government plans to penetrate Israeli market once diplomatic relations between the two countries was established.[22] Dato' Seri Dr. Mahathir Mohamad on June 19, 1994 admitted that he had several times corresponded with Israeli Prime Minister Yitzhak Rabin to discuss Malaysia's recognition of the Jewish state.[23] While Israel has recognized the new nation of Malaysia, Malaysia still not established diplomatic relations with the country.[24] The possibility of Malaysia established diplomatic relations with Israel cannot be separated from the government's attention since the Palestine Liberation Organization (PLO) signed the Declaration of Principles agreement with Israel on 13 September 1993. This is because both

---

[19] Anonymous, We can't protest over Israeli leader's visit Mahathir in *The Straits Times*, 26 October 1986, p. 12. See also Anonymous, Party Rakyat protests over Israeli leader in *The Straits Times*, 28 October 1986, p. 7.

[20] Anonymous, Tak akan bantah in *Berita Harian*, 27 October 1986, p. 6. See also Anonymous, Herzog visit: What MPs want to know in *The Straits Times*, 10 December 1986, p. 36. See also Anonymous, Why Herzog came - PLO man. What is still being said about the Herzog visit in *The Straits Times*, 14 December 1986, p. 14.

[21] Anonymous, Tentang Zionisme in *Berita Harian*, 12 December 1986, p. 8. See also Anonymous, BANTAH LAWATAN HERZOG in *Berita Harian*, 17 November 1986, p. 8. See also Anonymous, Mahathir tegur demo in *Berita Harian*, 30 November 1986, p. 1. See also Anonymous, Muhyiddin: Patuhi teguran Dr M in *Berita Harian*, 1 December 1986, p. 6. See also Anonymous, It's time to end all the fuss, says NST reader in *The Straits Times*, 16 December 1986, p. 9. See also Anonymous, Protests continue across Causeway in *The Business Times*, 19 November 1986, p. 18. See also Anonymous, Malaysians march to Causeway to protest Herzog visit in *The Business Times*, 29 November 1986, p. 1. See also Basir Siswo, Demo di Tambak Johor in *Berita Harian*, 29 November 1986, p. 9. See also Ismail Kassim, Dr. M: Envoy's recall won't affect ties. Protests held against Israeli President's visit to Singapore in *The Straits Times*, 17 November 1986, p. 1. See also Abu Mohd. Abduh, Why is Singapore Govt suddenly so arrogant? What Malaysians are still saying about the Herzog visit. Writer hints at secret relations with Israel in *The Straits Times*, 11 December 1986, p. 27. See also Asad Latif, The Herzog visit: Causeway over history in *The Business Times*, 19 December 1986, p. 8. See also Anonymous, Don't overdo protest action in *The Straits Times*, 5 December 1986, p. 31. See also Anonymous, Herzog's pending visit stirs up protests in KL in *The Business Times*, 15 November 1986, p. 12. See also MORE IN SORROW, Why pick Singapore as a whipping boy? Israeli leader's forthcoming visit in *The Straits Times*, 12 November 1986, p. 20. See also Anonymous, Forum. VIEWS ON HERZOG PROTESTS in *The Straits Times*, 2 December 1986, p. 2. See also Anonymous, P - jaya Tinggi KL dan Duta Indon balik ke sini in *Berita Harian*, 5 December 1986, p. 1. See also Anonymous, What are benefits if KL cuts links with Singapore? More reaction to the Herzog visit in *The Straits Times*, 21 December 1986, p. 15. See also LOVE THY NEIGHBOUR, Waste of time and money in *The Straits Times*, 2 December 1986, p. 13. See also LOYAL SINGAPOREAN, Be practical and realistic about defence in *The Straits Times*, 6 December 1986, p. 26.

[22] Anonymous, M'sia: Invest in Israel in *The New Paper*, 30 September 1993, p. 4. See also Anonymous, Malaysia 'to invest in Israel once ties are set up' in *The Straits Times*, 30 September 1993, p. 17.

[23] Anonymous, Dr M berutus surat dengan Rabin in *Berita Harian*, 20 June 1994, p. 2. See also Anonymous, Mahathir rules out ties with Israel till Palestine is settled in *The Straits Times*, 16 December 2000, p. 29. See also Anonymous, Mahathir gets letters from Rabin on diplomatic ties in *The Business Times*, 20 June 1994, p. 16.

[24] Anonymous, Pengakuan kepada S'pura in *Berita Harian*, 17 August 1965, p. 3.

countries will benefit economically if diplomatic relations were established.[25] However, the Cabinet wants to wait and see in advance how sincere Israel to comply with the peace agreement signed with the PLO before making a decision.[26] Tunku Abdullah Abdul Rahman trip, brother to Yang Di-Pertuan Agong of Malaysia and also the first from a senior officer of Malaysia to Israel in June 1994 was interpreted by the Israeli government as a first step that will eventually lead to diplomatic relations between the two countries. This is because Malaysia is considered as the most hostile country to Israel in Southeast Asia.[27] During this visit, he held talks with Israeli Prime Minister, Yithak Rabin[28] and find business opportunities in the country.[29]

There are also a number of Malaysian Minister that met Yitzhak Rabin in Paris in July 1994. The meeting was held in Yitzhak Rabin's accommodation hotel while he accept United Nations Educational, Scientific and Cultural Organisation (UNESCO) peace prize.[30] UMNO Youth movement on August 12, 1994 suggests fostering diplomatic relations with Israel as a sign of change in a more open attitude toward the Jewish state.[31] This follows the signing of a peace agreement between Israel and the PLO and Jordan.[32] According to Umno Youth chief, Rahim Tamby Chik, history has shown that Muslims and Jews can live together in peace from the time of Prophet Muhammad.[33] Dato' Seri Dr. Mahathir Mohamad reiterated on August 13, 1994 that Malaysia is still studying the possibility of establishing diplomatic relations with Israel even some Arab countries have done so. This is because the government has not satisfied the service of Israel against the Palestinian government.[34]

---

[25] Hawazi Daipi, Malaysia masih menanti saat yang sesuai in Berita Harian, 16 August 1994, p. 4.

[26] Anonymous, Malaysia 'not ready' for diplomatic ties with Israel in The Straits Times, 25 June 1994, p. 18.

[27] Anonymous, King's brother in Israel in The New Paper, 22 June 1994, p. 4. See also Anonymous, KL to act against King's kin in The New Paper, 25 July 1994, p. 20. See also Anonymous, Firm unaware of chairman's visit to Israel in The Straits Times, 22 June 1994, p. 17. See also Anonymous, King's brother visited Israel on business trip in The Straits Times, 22 June 1994, p. 17. See also Anonymous, KL govt to act against Agong's brother for Israel visit in The Straits Times, 26 July 1994, p. 2

[28] Anonymous, King's brother visited Israel: TV report in The Straits Times, 19 June 1994, p. 19.

[29] Anonymous, Trip to Israel was for business, says King's brother in The Straits Times, 17 July 1994, p. 21.

[30] Anonymous, Report: Some KL ministers met Rabin in The New Paper, 15 July 1994, p. 2.

[31] Anonymous, Malaysia's Umno youths call for ties with Israel in The Business Times, 13 August 1994, p. 3.

[32] Anonymous, Pemuda Umno mahu M'sia, Israel jalin ikatan in Berita Harian, 13 August 1994, p. 1.

[33] Anonymous, Consider ties with Israel, Umno Youth chief urges in The Straits Times, 13 August 1994, p. 20.

[34] Anonymous, KL masih timbang jalin hubungan dengan Israel in Berita Harian, 14 August 1994, p. 13. See also Anonymous, Malaysia needs time to consider setting up ties with Israel in The Straits Times, 14 September 1993, p. 8.

The Foreign Minister of Malaysia, Dato' Abdullah Ahmad Badawi in a press conference in Parliament on October 25, 1994 stating Malaysians irrespective of religion[35] who wish to worship at Masjid al-Aqsa in Jerusalem will be allowed to visit Israel even that country do not have diplomatic relations with Malaysia.[36] Malaysians intending to visit Jerusalem must get a special letter from the Immigration Department in advance, before they can be visited Jerusalem for a period of 14 days for religious purposes.[37] Malaysian government's decision to allow citizens to visit Jerusalem by the month of November 1994 not only welcomed by the people, but also by Israel. Israel's tourism commissioner in Jerusalem, Avi Liran welcomed the move and said all Malaysians regardless of religion are welcome to that place.[38] This was followed by the visit from Malaysian travel agents delegation and representatives of the ASEAN Tourism Association to Israel in April 1995 to review the potential joint venture.[39]

Deputy Director for Asia and the Pacific in the Israeli Foreign Ministry stated economic dividends of the Middle East peace process can have a positive impact on Asia. Israel also wants diplomatic relations with all ASEAN countries.[40] Following the positive progress since the peace agreement between the PLO and Israel, on January 13, 1996 Malaysian Cabinet has directed the Ministry of International Trade and Industry to look into the possibility of increasing trade with Israel in stages.[41] The private sector is also urged to forge trade ties with Israel.[42]

Bilateral trade between Malaysia and Israel has received support from the unexpected group. Ultra-Orthodox Jews or Haredi see Malaysia as a major source of cooking oil for the

---

[35] Anonymous, Jerusalem trips in *The New Paper*, 11 November 1994, p. 4.

[36] Anonymous, Malaysia izin rakyat lawat Israel bagi tujuan agama in *Berita Harian*, 26 October 1994, p. 1. See also Anonymous, Malaysians can visit Israel soon to pray at mosque in *The Straits Times*, 26 October 1994, p. 15.

[37] Anonymous, Surat khas diperlukan untuk ke Baitulmakdis in *Berita Harian*, 11 November 1994, p. 3. See also Anonymous, KL extends Jerusalem visits to non-Muslims in *The Straits Times*, 11 November 1994, p. 23.

[38] Anonymous, Ramai rakyat M'sia dijangka lawat Baitulmakdis in *Berita Harian*, 15 November 1994, p. 4. See also Anonymous, KL to broaden Jerusalem travel policy in *The Business Times*, 11 November 1994, p. 4.

[39] Anonymous, Malaysian travel agents visit Israel in *The Straits Times*, 1 April 1995, p. 22.

[40] Anonymous, Asia can gain from M-E peace: Israeli official in *The Business Times*, 11 January 1996, p. 3. See also Anonymous, Israel ready to expand ties in Asia, says official in *The Business Times*, 7 November 1992, p. 7. See also Anonymous, The lure of business cuts across culture and religion in *The Business Times*, 17 October 1994, p. 12.

[41] Anonymous, Ikatan dagang M'sia, Israel dikaji in *Berita Harian*, 14 January 1996, p. 9. See also Anonymous, KL to look into increasing trade links with Israel in *The Straits Times*, 14 January 1996, p. 2.

[42] Anonymous, Private sector urged to forge trade ties with Israel in *The Straits Times*, 17 January 1996, p. 19.

Easter holidays in a week.[43] Malaysia will boost its trade relations with Israel in an effort to get the country's new market in the Middle East. Parliamentary Secretary to the Ministry of International Trade and Industry, Dato' Hishammuddin Tun Hussein on June 7, 1996 indicated that the government will take a pragmatic and proactive approach to establishing trade relations with Israel.[44] He stated that the government is studying the possibility of sending trade team to Israel in an effort to dominate the Middle East market.[45]

The government has made a pragmatic and realistic step in establishing trade relations with Israel because Malaysia saw the country's potential as a catalyst for economic development in the Middle East following the Arab-Israel peace treaty.[46] Israeli private companies also allowed to invest in Labuan, which was promoted as an International Offshore Financial Centre.[47] Any form of relations with Israel at any stage or form is dependent on whether the government is satisfied or not with the role played by the Israeli government in ensuring peace talks in the Middle East a success.[48] According to the Secretary General of the Foreign Ministry, Tan Sri Ahmad Kamil, Malaysia is in no hurry to establish diplomatic relations with Israel. It will only do so after the ongoing peace process between Israel and Syria completed.[49] Dato' Seri Dr. Mahathir further stated Islamic countries should not fight against Israel or among themselves to resolve the Arab-Israeli crisis.[50] He urged Muslims to use the power of the mind and not merely strength against Israel and turn the more than half a century defeat.[51]

On March 24, 1997, Dato' Seri Dr. Mahathir Mohamad state Malaysian government's decision to allow the Israeli cricket team participated in international tournament here is to make them realize that people of different races and religions can live together in peace in a country like Malaysia.[52] Deputy Prime Minister of Malaysia, Dato' Seri Anwar Ibrahim state

---

[43] Anonymous, Jewish group turns to Malaysia for cooking oil in *The Straits Times*, 3 May 1997, p. 23.

[44] Anonymous, M'sia tingkat dagang dengan Israel in *Berita Harian*, 8 June 1996, p. 18.

[45] Anonymous, Trade team 'may visit Israel' in *The Straits Times*, 8 June 1996, p. 23.

[46] Anonymous, Malaysia sees Israel as economic catalyst in Mid-East in *The Straits Times*, 16 July 1997, p. 27.

[47] Anonymous, Private Israeli firms given go-ahead to invest in Labuan in *The Straits Times*, 18 April 1997, p. 37.

[48] Anonymous, Ties with Israel depend on peace moves: Minister in *The Straits Times*, 22 June 1996, p. 26.

[49] Anonymous, Ties with Israel after proof of peace in *The New Paper*, 27 January 1996, p. 21. See also Anonymous, KL-Israel ties 'only after peace accord with Syria' in *The Straits Times*, 28 January 1996, p. 24.

[50] Anonymous, Fighting Israel 'not the way to solve conflict' in *The Straits Times*, 7 December 1996, p. 42.

[51] Anonymous, Mahathir syor guna fikiran untuk atasi Israel in *Berita Harian*, 17 October 2003, p. 16.

political parties should not mix politics with sport. According to him, sport association from any country whatsoever is excluded from political and had nothing to do with politics.[53] This step is getting resistance from the opposition party, the Islamic Party of Malaysia (PAS) and several non-governmental organizations (NGOs).[54] PAS warned on March 31, 1997 that they will act violently in the future to prevent a cricket match with Israeli team after two previously demonstrating actions failed.[55] PAS also having similar protest when Israeli cricket team visits Malaysia again in 2000.[56]

On October 13, 1997, Malaysia's Minister of Tourism, Arts and Culture, Dato' Sabbarudin Chik defends Dato' Seri Dr. Mahathir Mohamad over the fact associating Jews with the financial problems of his country and Malaysia rejects accusations of anti-Semitism.[57] On 30 September 1999, the Foreign Minister of Malaysia, Dato' Seri Syed Hamid Albar was subjected to PAS criticism because held an informal meeting with Israeli Foreign Minister, David Levy in the headquarters of the United Nations. PAS described Israel as a terrorist state and the meeting was humiliating Muslims.[58] However, according to Deputy Prime Minister, Dato' Seri Abdullah Ahmad Badawi, the relationship between Malaysia and Israel will not change just because the meeting.[59]

---

[52] Anonymous, Malaysia undang pasukan kriket Israel in *Berita Harian*, 24 March 1997, p. 2.

[53] Anonymous, Anwar: Usah campur politik dengan sukan in *Berita Harian*, 27 March 1997, p. 8.

[54] Anonymous, Demo bantah pasukan Israel in *Berita Harian*, 26 March 1997, p. 1. See also Carolyn Hong, Sensitive issue in *The Straits Times*, 16 February 2005, p. 15. See also Anonymous, Varsity students join cricket protest in *The Straits Times*, 5 April 1997, p. 20.

[55] Anonymous, PAS ugut tindak ganas ke atas pasukan Israel in *Berita Harian*, 1 April 1997, p. 1. See also Anonymous, Demo anti-Israel cemar nama Islam in *Berita Harian*, 12 April 1997, p. 8. See also Anonymous, Protest over Israeli cricket team in KL in *The Straits Times*, 26 March 1997, p. 3. See also Anonymous, 'This is stupid' in *The New Paper*, 5 April 1997, p. 2. See also Anonymous, Free anti-Israel protesters: Muslim groups in *The Straits Times*, 7 April 1997, p. 18. See also Anonymous, KL tahan 49 selepas bantahan anti-Israel in *Berita Harian*, 5 April 1997, p. 1. See also Anonymous, Act against anti-Israel protesters: Umno Youth in *The Straits Times*, 9 April 1997, p. 23. See also Anonymous, KL police break up anti-Israel protest in *The Straits Times*, 5 April 1997, p. 1. See also Brendan Pereira, Anti-Israeli-cricket students to protest against 'unfair' fine in *The Straits Times*, 26 April 1997, p. 35.

[56] Anonymous, Protest and drama as PAS man is freed in *Today*, 9 December 2000, p. 1.

[57] Anonymous, 'Malaysia tidak anti-Yahudi' in *Berita Harian*, 14 October 1997, p. 2. See also Anonymous, Amerika bidas ulasan Mahathir atas isu Yahudi in *Berita Harian*, 17 October 1997, p. 3.

[58] Anonymous, PAS kecam Hamid kerana runding dengan Israel in *Berita Harian*, 1 October 1999, p. 13. See also Anonymous, PAS twisted facts of Israeli meet: Minister in *The Straits Times*, 8 October 1999, p. 46. See also Anonymous, Historic meeting between KL, Israel ministers in *The Straits Times*, 28 September 1999, p. 2. See aslo Anonymous, Minister criticised for contact with Israel in *The Straits Times*, 1 October 1999, p. 52. See also Carolyn Hong, Sensitive issue in *The Straits Times*, 16 February 2005, p. 15. See also Anonymous, Levy talks with Syed Hamid 'informal' in *The Straits Times*, 30 September 1999, p. 26.

[59] Anonymous, No change in ties with Israel in *The Straits Times*, 5 October 1999, p. 29.

Malaysia's General Election Campaign in 1999 was marred in controversy when the opposition line began spreading a letter signed by Prime Minister, showed Barisan Nasional (BN) sought the cooperation of Israeli leaders to seek funds to finance election campaigns.[60] Subsequently in February 2000, PAS also demanded the Malaysian government to expel the Israeli tennis team from the country. The Israeli women and men team were in Malaysia to participate in the World Team Table Tennis Championship in Kuala Lumpur since February 20.[61] The Malaysian government mantain the Israeli Table Tennis team presence by stating that Malaysia cannot afford to discriminate against any country if it wants to host international sporting events.[62] There are also anti-Israel demonstration of about 300 people on October 8, 1999 that act burning the flag of Barisan Nasional (BN) as a protest meeting between the two Foreign Ministers of Malaysia and Israel in the United States. The protesters were made up of university students and locals.[63] Dato' Seri Dr. Mahathir Mohamad expressed concern on June 20, 2002 about the safety of the supporters of Israel out of the target of a terrorist attack in any part of the world if there is no in-depth explanation about the Middle East crisis.[64]

In March 2005, five non-governmental leaders from Israel visiting Malaysia to attend a conference on Middle East peace.[65] On December 19, 2006, Israel launched a Malay-Indonesia language website in an effort to improve relations with Muslims in Indonesia and Malaysia.[66] In May 2007, the Minister of Foreign Affairs of Singapore, George Yeo said Malaysia and Indonesia is no longer expressed dissatisfaction against Singapore's move to enhance its bilateral relations with Israel because of the world situation has changed and the main focus now is to address the threat of global terrorism and conflict Sunni-Shia conflict in the Middle East.[67] Deputy Prime Minister of Malaysia, Dato' Seri Najib Tun Razak stated the Ministry of Defence realized that Singapore and Israel have established good relationships covering the areas of defense equipment. However, the Malaysian government believes it will

---

[60] Anonymous, 'Surat BN' minta kerjasama Israel disebar in *Berita Harian*, 25 November 1999, p. 12.

[61] Anonymous, PAS gesa KL usir pasukan pingpong Israel in *Berita Harian*, 24 February 2000, p. 9. See also Anonymous, PAS demands expulsion of Israeli table-tennis team in *The Straits Times*, 24 February 2000, p. 35.

[62] Anonymous, KL defends presence of Israeli team in *The Straits Times*, 27 February 2000, p. 25.

[63] Anonymous, 300 sertai tunjuk perasaan anti Israel di KL in *Berita Harian*, 9 October 1999, p. 20.

[64] Anonymous, Krisis Timur Tengah: Perlu ada huraian in *Berita Harian*, 21 June 2002, p. 12.

[65] Carolyn Hong, PAS pulls out of meeting because of Israelis in *The Straits Times*, 23 March 2005, p. 13.

[66] Anonymous, Israel lancar laman web bahasa Melayu-Indonesia in *Berita Harian*, 20 December 2006, p. 7.

[67] Anonymous, Sebab M'sia, Indon tidak bantah in *Berita Harian*, 3 May 2007, p. 3.

not affect the region.[68] On 1 April 2008, the Malaysian government is willing to grant an exemption to the anti-Israel visa policy for two Israelis, coach Avram Grant and midfielder Tal Ben Haim in the Chelsea football team due to their threats to cancel football matches here.[69] Malaysia's Ministry of Home Affairs also will not prevent the two Israelis from entering the country for Chelsea pre-season tour because they do not want to interfere in any sporting event.[70] The Foreign Ministry also had no objection to the coming together of that two Israelis with Chelsea.[71]

---

[68] Anonymous, KL: Ikatan Singapura-Israel tidak jejas rantau in Berita Harian, 30 June 2007, p. 17.

[69] Anonymous, KL MAY ISSUE VISAS TO BLUES' ISRAELIS in *The Straits Times*, 1 April 2008, p. 36.

[70] Anonymous, M'sia has no problem with Chelsea visit in *Today*, 28 April 2008, p. 43. See also Anonymous, M'sia has no problem with Chelsea visit in *Today* (Afternoon Edition), 28 April 2008, p. 43.

[71] Anonymous, Okey walau ada ahli Yahudi in *Berita Harian*, 15 April 2008, p. 6.

Reference

Archive File

File of Jabatan Arkib Negara Malaysia, *Unforgettable Moments Recorded During- The Asian Football Cup Finals - 1964 Presented To Tunku Abdul Rahman Putra (President, A.F.C. by The Israel Football Association, Tel - Aviv, 3.6.1964.*, Para pengurus dan pemain-pemain yang mengambil bahagian selamat tiba di Tel -AAviv pada 3.6.1964.Bagi The Asian Football Cup Finals 1964, 3 June 1964.

File of Jabatan Arkib Negara Malaysia, *Unforgettable Moments Recorded During- The Asian Football Cup Finals - 1964 Presented To Tunku Abdul Rahman Putra (President, A.F.C. by The Israel Football Association, Tel - Aviv, 3.6.1964.*, Para Pengurus dan pemain dari Korea yang mengambil bahagian Teh Asia Football Cup di Tel-Aviv pada 3.6.1964 selamat mendarat di negara itu dan disambut dengan jambangan bunga., 3 June 1964.

File of Jabatan Arkib Negara Malaysia, *Unforgettable Moments Recorded During- The Asian Football Cup Finals - 1964 Presented To Tunku Abdul Rahman Putra (President, A.F.C. by The Israel Football Association, Tel - Aviv, 3.6.1964.*, Pasukan yang mengambil bahagian - The Asian Football Cup Finals bergambar ramai di Tel - Aviv, 3.5.1964., 3 May 1964.

File of Jabatan Arkib Negara Malaysia, *Unforgettable Moments Recorded During- The Asian Football Cup Finals - 1964 Presented To Tunku Abdul Rahman Putra (President, A.F.C. by The Israel Football Association, Tel - Aviv, 3.6.1964.*, Tan Sri Hamzah Abu Samah bergambar dengan pengurus-pengurus pasukan yang mengambil bahagian - The Asian Football Cup Finals - Tel-Aviv pada 3.6.1964., 3 June 1964.

File of Jabatan Arkib Negara Malaysia, *Unforgettable Moments Recorded During- The Asian Football Cup Finals - 1964 Presented To Tunku Abdul Rahman Putra (President, A.F.C. by The Israel Football Association, Tel - Aviv, 3.6.1964.*, Wakil-wakil Pengurus bagi negara yang mengambil bahagian bergambar ramai di pejabat semasa The Asian Football Cup Finals, Tel-Aviv, 3.6.1964., 3 June 1964.

File of Jabatan Arkib Negara Malaysia, *Unforgettable Moments Recorded During- The Asian Football Cup Finals - 1964 Presented To Tunku Abdul Rahman Putra (President, A.F.C. by The Israel Football Association, Tel - Aviv, 3.6.1964.*, Pengurus-pengurus bagi negara-negara yang mengambil bahagian bergambar ramai di Dewan ketika menghadiri The Asian Football Cup Finals 1964 di Tel -Aviv., no date.

File of Jabatan Arkib Negara Malaysia, *Unforgettable Moments Recorded During- The Asian Football Cup Finals - 1964 Presented To Tunku Abdul Rahman Putra (President, A.F.C. by The Israel Football Association, Tel - Aviv, 3.6.1964.*, Pengurus dari Tel Aviv sedang berucap semasa wakil-wakil negara hadir bagi The Asian Football Cup Final pada tahun 1964., no date.

File of Jabatan Arkib Negara Malaysia, *Unforgettable Moments Recorded During- The Asian Football Cup Finals - 1964 Presented To Tunku Abdul Rahman Putra (President, A.F.C. by The Israel Football Association, Tel - Aviv, 3.6.1964.*, Pengurus-pengurus dari negara-negara yang mengambil bahagian bergambar ramai semasa berkumpul di Tel-Aviv pada 1964 bagi The Asian Football Cup Finals., no date.

File of Jabatan Arkib Negara Malaysia, *Unforgettable Moments Recorded During- The Asian Football Cup Finals - 1964 Presented To Tunku Abdul Rahman Putra (President, A.F.C. by The Israel Football Association, Tel - Aviv, 3.6.1964.*, Pegawai-pegawai bagi negara-negara yang mengambil bahagian The Asian Football Cup Finals 1964 di Tel Aviv bergambar ramai sebagai kenang-kenangan., no date.

File of Jabatan Arkib Negara Malaysia, *Unforgettable Moments Recorded During- The Asian Football Cup Finals - 1964 Presented To Tunku Abdul Rahman Putra (President, A.F.C. by The Israel Football Association, Tel - Aviv, 3.6.1964.*, Pengurus-pengurus yang mengambil bahagian The Asian Football Cup Finals 1964 sedang berbincang, no date.

File of Jabatan Arkib Negara Malaysia, *Unforgettable Moments Recorded During- The Asian Football Cup Finals - 1964 Presented To Tunku Abdul Rahman Putra (President, A.F.C. by The Israel Football Association, Tel - Aviv, 3.6.1964.*, Tan Sri Hamzah Abu Samah sedang bersantai bersama-sama dengan rakan-rakan di Tel-Aviv pada 1964, sempena The Asian Football Cup Finals., no date.
File of Jabatan Arkib Negara Malaysia, *Unforgettable Moments Recorded During- The Asian Football Cup Finals - 1964 Presented To Tunku Abdul Rahman Putra (President, A.F.C. by The Israel Football Association, Tel - Aviv, 3.6.1964.*, Pasukan Korea dan lawannya sedang beraksi dipadang sempena The Asian Football Cup Finals di Tel Aviv pada 1964., no date.

File of Jabatan Arkib Negara Malaysia, *Unforgettable Moments Recorded During- The Asian Football Cup Finals - 1964 Presented To Tunku Abdul Rahman Putra (President, A.F.C. by The Israel Football Association, Tel - Aviv, 3.6.1964.*, Pemain-pemain yang mengambil bahagian sedang beraksi di padang dalam perlawanan The Asian Football Cup Finals di Tel - Aviv 1964., no date.

File of Jabatan Arkib Negara Malaysia, *Unforgettable Moments Recorded During- The Asian Football Cup Finals - 1964 Presented To Tunku Abdul Rahman Putra (President, A.F.C. by The Israel Football Association, Tel - Aviv, 3.6.1964.*, Bendera-bendera yang mengambil bahagian dalam The Asian Football Cup Finals - 1964 di Tel-Aviv sedang dijulang sempena perasmian., no date.

File of Jabatan Arkib Negara Malaysia, *Unforgettable Moments Recorded During- The Asian Football Cup Finals - 1964 Presented To Tunku Abdul Rahman Putra (President, A.F.C. by The Israel Football Association, Tel - Aviv, 3.6.1964.*, Bendera-bendera negara yang mengambil bahagian diarak keliling padang sempena perasmian The Asian Football Cup Finals - 1964 di Tel - Aviv., no date.

File of Jabatan Arkib Negara Malaysia, *Unforgettable Moments Recorded During- The Asian Football Cup Finals - 1964 Presented To Tunku Abdul Rahman Putra (President, A.F.C. by The Israel Football Association, Tel - Aviv, 3.6.1964.*, Bendera-bendera yang mengambil bahagian sedang berkibar di tengah padang sempena perasmian The Asian Football Cup Finals 1964 di Tel-Aviv., no date.

File of Jabatan Arkib Negara Malaysia, *Unforgettable Moments Recorded During- The Asian Football Cup Finals - 1964 Presented To Tunku Abdul Rahman Putra (President, A.F.C. by*

The Israel Football Association, Tel - Aviv, 3.6.1964., Pasukan yang berjaya sedang menjulang piala dan mengibar bendera mengelilingi padang sempena The Asian Football Cup Finals - 1964., no date.

File of Jabatan Arkib Negara Malaysia, *Unforgettable Moments Recorded During- The Asian Football Cup Finals - 1964 Presented To Tunku Abdul Rahman Putra (President, A.F.C. by The Israel Football Association, Tel - Aviv, 3.6.1964.*, Pemain No. 8 sedang menerima hadiah dalam perlawanan The Asian Football Cup Finals - 1964 di Tel - Aviv., no date.

File of Jabatan Arkib Negara Malaysia, *Unforgettable Moments Recorded During- The Asian Football Cup Finals - 1964 Presented To Tunku Abdul Rahman Putra (President, A.F.C. by The Israel Football Association, Tel - Aviv, 3.6.1964.*, Pasukan dari India sedang menjulang piala kemenangan dan bergambar ramai sempena The Asian Football Cup Finals - 1964 di Tel- Aviv., no date.

Newspaper

Abul Fazil. 1966. Allegations not true, says Israeli businessman. *The Straits Times*, 14 January 1966: 11.

Abu Mohd. Abduh. 1986. Why is Singapore Govt suddenly so arrogant? What Malaysians are still saying about the Herzog visit. Writer hints at secret relations with Israel. *The Straits Times*, 11 December: 27.

Anonymous. 1962. Israel's Malaysia hopes. SHE SEES GOOD IMMEDIATE PROSPECTS FOR HER VARIOUS GARMENTS AND CANNED FOODSTUFFS. *The Straits Times*, 14 September: 16.

Anonymous. 1964. PAS na' minta tarek akuan kpd Israel. *Berita Harian*, 13 August: 5.

Anonymous. 1964. 'KERAJAAN' ISRAEL BELUM DI-I'TIRAF. *Berita Harian*, 26 November: 5.

Anonymous. 1964. Hubongan dgn Israel: Amaran kpd pembangkang. 'Tudohan2 liar boleh menimbulkan salah faham yg menyukarkan'. *Berita Harian*, 12 December: 5.

Anonymous. 1965. Seruan menarek balek pengakuan kapada Israel. *Berita Harian*, 14 March: 10.
Anonymous. 1965. 'Withdraw Israel recognition'. *The Straits Times*, 14 March: 7.

Anonymous. 1965. UMNO Arau seru pengakuan kepada Israel di-batalkan. *Berita Harian*, 26 March: 8.

Anonymous. 1965. Pengakuan kepada S'pura. *Berita Harian*, 17 August: 3.

Anonymous. 1966. Israeli trader is expelled. He indulged in local politics, says Tengku. *The Straits Times*, 13 January: 1.

Anonymous. 1966. MENGAPA SAUDAGAR ISRAEL DI-SUROH KELUAR. *Berita Harian*, 22 March 1966: 5.

Anonymous. 1966. Imej Malaysia: Asri hendak berjumpa Tun. *Berita Harian*, 14 May: 3.

Anonymous. 1967. BELAJAR-LAH DARI ISRAEL, KATA TOKOH UMNO. *Berita Harian*, 11 June: 1.

Anonymous. 1974. Imports from Israel almost at standstill. *The Straits Times*, 8 March: 17.

Anonymous. 1979. Malaysia hails pact. *The Straits Times*, 28 March: 3.

Anonymous. 1985. Sorry about that — TV3. *The Straits Times*, 18 April: 40.

Anonymous. 1986. We can't protest over Israeli leader's visit Mahathir. *The Straits Times*, 26 October: 12.

Anonymous. 1986. Tak akan bantah. *Berita Harian*, 27 October: 6.

Anonymous. 1986. Party Rakyat protests over Israeli leader. *The Straits Times*, 28 October: 7.

Anonymous. 1986. 'KL won't recall envoy during Herzog visit'. *The Straits Times*, 8 November: 30.
Anonymous. 1986. KL tak akan bertindak. *Berita Harian*, 9 November: 2.

Anonymous. 1986. Herzog's pending visit stirs up protests in KL. *The Business Times*, 15 November: 12.

Anonymous. 1986. KL-Singapore relations intact, assures Dr M. *The Business Times*, 17 November: 1.

Anonymous. 1986. BANTAH LAWATAN HERZOG. *Berita Harian*, 17 November: 8.

Anonymous. 1986. Republic should heed Malaysians' views: Hussein. *The Straits Times*, 19 November: 12.

Anonymous. 1986. Protests continue across Causeway. *The Business Times*, 19 November: 18.

Anonymous. 1986. Johor 'has no mandate to decide on ties review'. *The Straits Times*, 20 November: 13.

Anonymous. 1986. Malaysians march to Causeway to protest Herzog visit. *The Business Times*, 29 November: 1.

Anonymous. 1986. Mahathir tegur demo. *Berita Harian*, 30 November: 1.

Anonymous. 1986. Muhyiddin: Patuhi teguran Dr M. *Berita Harian*, 1 December: 6.

Anonymous. 1986. Forum. VIEWS ON HERZOG PROTESTS. *The Straits Times*, 2 December: 2.

Anonymous. 1986. P - jaya Tinggi KL dan Duta Indon balik ke sini. *Berita Harian*, 5 December: 1.

Anonymous. 1986. Don't overdo protest action. *The Straits Times*, 5 December: 31.

Anonymous. 1986. Malaysia hanya tentang Zionisme . *Berita Harian*, 6 December: 1.

Anonymous. 1986. Malaysia opposes Zionism, not Israel or Jewish people, says Rais Yatim. *The Business Times*, 6 December: 12.

Anonymous. 1986. Rais: Govt opposes Zionism, not Jews. *The Straits Times*, 6 December: 13.

Anonymous. 1986. Herzog visit: What MPs want to know. *The Straits Times*, 10 December: 36.

Anonymous. 1986. Tentang Zionisme. *Berita Harian*, 12 December: 8.

Anonymous. 1986. Why Herzog came - PLO man. What is still being said about the Herzog visit. *The Straits Times*, 14 December: 14.

Anonymous. 1986. It's time to end all the fuss, says NST reader. *The Straits Times*, 16 December: 9.

Anonymous. 1986. What are benefits if KL cuts links with Singapore? More reaction to the Herzog visit. *The Straits Times*, 21 December: 15.

Anonymous. 1992. Israel ready to expand ties in Asia, says official. *The Business Times*, 7 November: 7.

Anonymous. 1993. Malaysia needs time to consider setting up ties with Israel. *The Straits Times*, 14 September: 8.

Anonymous. 1993. M'sia: Invest in Israel. *The New Paper*, 30 September: 4.

Anonymous. 1993. Malaysia 'to invest in Israel once ties are set up'. *The Straits Times*, 30 September: 17.

Anonymous. 1994. King's brother visited Israel: TV report. *The Straits Times*, 19 June: 19.
Anonymous. 1994. Dr M berutus surat dengan Rabin. *Berita Harian*, 20 June: 2.

Anonymous. 1994. Mahathir gets letters from Rabin on diplomatic ties. *The Business Times*, 20 June: 16.

Anonymous. 1994. King's brother in Israel. *The New Paper*, 22 June: 4.

Anonymous. 1994. Firm unaware of chairman's visit to Israel. *The Straits Times*, 22 June: 17.

Anonymous. 1994. King's brother visited Israel on business trip. *The Straits Times*, 22 June: 17.

Anonymous. 1994. Malaysia 'not ready' for diplomatic ties with Israel. *The Straits Times*, 25 June: 18.

Anonymous. 1994. Report: Some KL ministers met Rabin. *The New Paper*, 15 July: 2.

Anonymous. 1994. Trip to Israel was for business, says King's brother. *The Straits Times*, 17 July: 21.

Anonymous. 1994. KL to act against King's kin. *The New Paper*, 25 July: 20.

Anonymous. 1994. KL govt to act against Agong's brother for Israel visit. *The Straits Times*, 26 July: 2.

Anonymous. 1994. Malaysia's Umno youths call for ties with Israel. *The Business Times*, 13 August: 3.

Anonymous. 1994. Pemuda Umno mahu M'sia, Israel jalin ikatan. *Berita Harian*, 13 August: 1.

Anonymous. 1994. Consider ties with Israel, Umno Youth chief urges. *The Straits Times*, 13 August: 20.

Anonymous. 1994. KL masih timbang jalin hubungan dengan Israel. *Berita Harian*, 14 August: 13.

Anonymous. 1994. The lure of business cuts across culture and religion. *The Business Times*, 17 October: 12.

Anonymous. 1994. Malaysia izin rakyat lawat Israel bagi tujuan agama. *Berita Harian*, 26 October: 1.

Anonymous. 1994. Malaysians can visit Israel soon to pray at mosque. *The Straits Times*, 26 October: 15.

Anonymous. 1994. Jerusalem trips. *The New Paper*, 11 November: 4.

Anonymous. 1994. Surat khas diperlukan untuk ke Baitulmakdis. *Berita Harian*, 11 November: 3.

Anonymous. 1994. KL extends Jerusalem visits to non-Muslims. *The Straits Times*, 11 November: 23.

Anonymous. 1994. KL to broaden Jerusalem travel policy. *The Business Times*, 11 November: 4.

Anonymous. 1994. Ramai rakyat M'sia dijangka lawat Baitulmakdis. *Berita Harian*, 15 November: 4.

Anonymous. 1995. Malaysian travel agents visit Israel. *The Straits Times*, 1 April: 22.

Anonymous. 1996. Asia can gain from M-E peace: Israeli official. *The Business Times*, 11 January: 3.

Anonymous. 1996. KL to look into increasing trade links with Israel. *The Straits Times*, 14 January: 2.

Anonymous. 1996. Ikatan dagang M'sia, Israel dikaji dlm. *Berita Harian*, 14 January: 9.

Anonymous. 1996. Private sector urged to forge trade ties with Israel. *The Straits Times*, 17 January: 19.

Anonymous. 1996. Ties with Israel after proof of peace. *The New Paper*, 27 January: 21.

Anonymous. 1996. KL-Israel ties 'only after peace accord with Syria'. *The Straits Times*, 28 January: 24.

Anonymous. 1996. M'sia tingkat dagang dengan Israel. *Berita Harian*, 8 June: 18.

Anonymous. 1996. Trade team 'may visit Israel'. *The Straits Times*, 8 June: 23.

Anonymous. 1996. Ties with Israel depend on peace moves: Minister. *The Straits Times*, 22 June: 26.

Anonymous. 1996. Fighting Israel 'not the way to solve conflict'. *The Straits Times*, 7 December: 42.

Anonymous. 1997. Malaysia undang pasukan kriket Israel. *Berita Harian*, 24 March: 2.

Anonymous. 1997. Demo bantah pasukan Israel. *Berita Harian*, 26 March: 1.

Anonymous. 1997. Protest over Israeli cricket team in KL. *The Straits Times*, 26 March: 3.

Anonymous. 1997. Anwar: Usah campur politik dengan sukan. *Berita Harian*, 27 March: 8.

Anonymous. 1997. PAS ugut tindak ganas ke atas pasukan Israel. *Berita Harian*, 1 April: 1.

Anonymous. 1997. KL police break up anti-Israel protest. *The Straits Times*, 5 April: 1.

Anonymous. 1997. 'This is stupid'. *The New Paper*, 5 April: 2.

Anonymous. 1997. KL tahan 49 selepas bantahan anti-Israel. *Berita Harian*, 5 April: 1.

Anonymous. 1997. Varsity students join cricket protest. *The Straits Times*, 5 April: 20.

Anonymous. 1997. Free anti-Israel protesters: Muslim groups. *The Straits Times*, 7 April: 18.

Anonymous. 1997. Act against anti-Israel protesters: Umno Youth. *The Straits Times*, 9 April: 23.

Anonymous. 1997. Demo anti-Israel cemar nama Islam. *Berita Harian*, 12 April: 8.

Anonymous. 1997. Private Israeli firms given go-ahead to invest in Labuan. *The Straits Times*, 18 April: 37.

Anonymous. 1997. Jewish group turns to Malaysia for cooking oil. *The Straits Times*, 3 May: 23.

Anonymous. 1997. Malaysia sees Israel as economic catalyst in Mid-East. *The Straits Times*, 16 July: 27.

Anonymous. 1997. 'Malaysia tidak anti-Yahudi'. *Berita Harian*, 14 October: 2.

Anonymous. 1997. Amerika bidas ulasan Mahathir atas isu Yahudi. *Berita Harian*, 17 October: 3.

Anonymous. 1999. Historic meeting between KL, Israel ministers. *The Straits Times*, 28 September: 2.

Anonymous. 1999. Levy talks with Syed Hamid 'informal'. *The Straits Times*, 30 September: 26.

Anonymous. 1999. PAS kecam Hamid kerana runding dengan Israel. *Berita Harian*, 1 October: 13.

Anonymous. 1999. Minister criticised for contact with Israel. *The Straits Times*, 1 October: 52.

Anonymous. 1999. No change in ties with Israel. *The Straits Times*, 5 October: 29.

Anonymous. 1999. PAS twisted facts of Israeli meet: Minister. *The Straits Times*, 8 October: 46.

Anonymous. 1999. 300 sertai tunjuk perasaan anti Israel di KL. *Berita Harian*, 9 October: 20.

Anonymous. 1999. 'Surat BN' minta kerjasama Israel disebar. *Berita Harian*, 25 November: 12.

Anonymous. 2000. PAS gesa KL usir pasukan pingpong Israel. *Berita Harian*, 24 February: 9.

Anonymous. 2000. PAS demands expulsion of Israeli table-tennis team. *The Straits Times*, 24 February: 35.

Anonymous. 2000. KL defends presence of Israeli team. *The Straits Times*, 27 February: 25.

Anonymous. 2000. Protest and drama as PAS man is freed. *Today*, 9 December: 1.

Anonymous. 2000. Mahathir rules out ties with Israel till Palestine is settled. *The Straits Times*, 16 December: 29.

Anonymous. 2002. Krisis Timur Tengah: Perlu ada huraian. *Berita Harian*, 21 June: 12.

Anonymous. 2003. Mahathir syor guna fikiran untuk atasi Israel. *Berita Harian*, 17 October: 16.

Anonymous. 2006. Israel lancar laman web bahasa Melayu-Indonesia. *Berita Harian*, 20 December: 7.

Anonymous. 2007. Sebab M'sia, Indon tidak bantah. *Berita Harian*, 3 May: 3.

Anonymous. 2007. KL: Ikatan Singapura-Israel tidak jejas rantau. Berita Harian, 30 June: 17.

Anonymous. 2008. KL MAY ISSUE VISAS TO BLUES' ISRAELIS. *The Straits Times*, 1 April: 36.

Anonymous. 2008. Okey walau ada ahli Yahudi. *Berita Harian*, 15 April: 6.

Anonymous. 2008. M'sia has no problem with Chelsea visit. *Today*, 28 April: 43.

Anonymous. 2008. M'sia has no problem with Chelsea visit. *Today* (Afternoon Edition), 28 April: 43.

Asad Latif. 1986. The Herzog visit: Causeway over history. *The Business Times*, 19 December: 8.

Basir Siswo. 1986. Demo di Tambak Johor. *Berita Harian*, 29 November: 9.

Brendan Pereira. 1997. Anti-Israeli-cricket students to protest against 'unfair' fine. *The Straits Times*, 26 April: 35.

Carolyn Hong. 2005. Sensitive issue. *The Straits Times*, 16 February: 15.

Carolyn Hong. 2005. PAS pulls out of meeting because of Israelis. *The Straits Times*, 23 March: 13.

Firdaus Abdullah & Allas Ali. 1964. 'KITA ANTI-KEKERASAN'. Tengku menerangkan: Kita mengakui Israel tapi tidak ada perhubungan. *Berita Harian*, 4 December: 5.

Hawazi Daipi. 1994. Malaysia masih menanti saat yang sesuai. *Berita Harian*, 16 August: 4.

Ismail Kassim. 1986. Dr. M: Envoy's recall won't affect ties. Protests held against Israeli President's visit to Singapore. *The Straits Times*, 17 November: 1.
LOVE THY NEIGHBOUR. 1986. Waste of time and money. *The Straits Times*, 2 December: 13.

LOYAL SINGAPOREAN. 1986. Be practical and realistic about defence. *The Straits Times*, 6 December: 26.

Mazlan Nordin. 1965. Tengku kecham pemimpin2 PAS di-Dewan Ra'ayat . Jangan membuat tudohan bukan2 atas dasar luar. *Berita Harian*, 26 November: 5.

MORE IN SORROW. 1986. Why pick Singapore as a whipping boy? Israeli leader's forthcoming visit. *The Straits Times*, 12 November: 20.

Our Parliamentary Reporters. 1964. Relations with Israel? Denial by Tengku and a word of caution… Opposition MPs warned of the risk of 'a lot of misunderstanding' with Arab countries. *The Straits Times*, 12 December: 8.

Thalatha. 1966. Malaysia tidak pernah akui negara Israel. *Berita Harian*, 24 August: 5.

Journal

Moshe Yegar. 2006. Malaysia: Anti-Semitism without Jews. *Jewish Political Studies Review* 18: 3-4.

Book

Jacob Abadi. 2003. *Israel's Quest for Recognition and Acceptance in Asia: Garrison State Diplomacy*. London: Frank Cass.